PIONEER VALLEY EDUCATIONAL PRESS, INC.

HARD AND
SOFT

RUTH MATTISON

T5-DHA-402

Here is a rock.
The rock is hard.

Here is a blanket.
The blanket is soft.

Here is a floor.

The floor is hard.

Here is a bed.

The bed is soft.

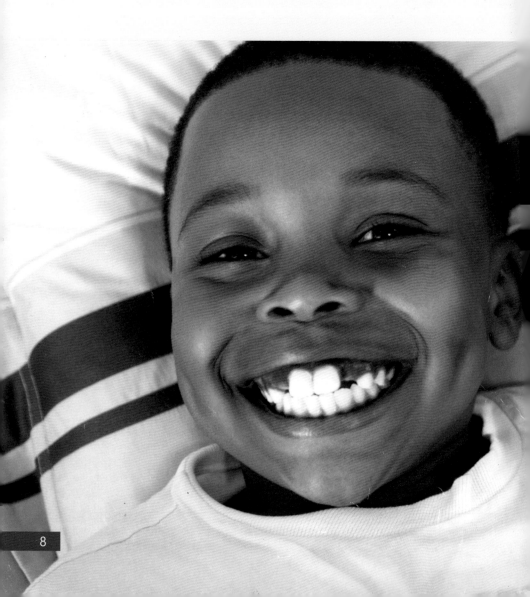

Here is a wall.
The wall is hard.

Here is a rabbit.
The rabbit is soft.

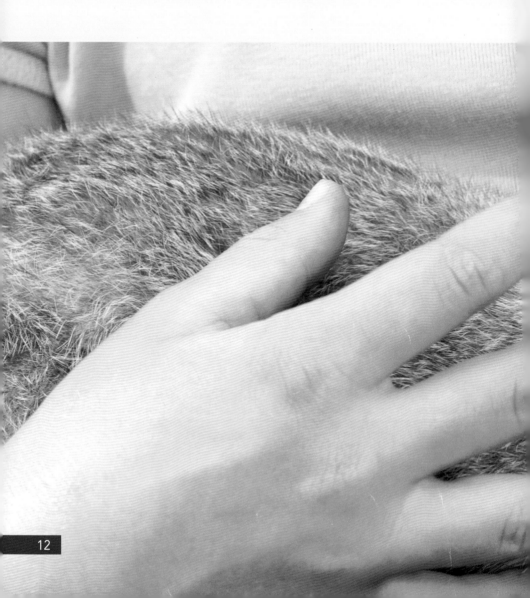

Here is a bowling ball.
The bowling ball is hard.

soft
blanket

soft
rabbit

soft
bed

hard
bowling ball

hard
rock

hard
floor

hard
wall